alterations

alterations

GEORGE PAYERLE

George Amabile, Editor

Signature
EDITIONS

Cover design by Terry Gallagher/Doowah Design.
Cover painting, *Sighting*, © 2004, Deborah DeWit Marchant.
Photo of George Payerle by Maggie Scherf.

This book was printed on Ancient Forest Friendly paper.
Printed and bound in Canada by AGMV Marquis Imprimeur Inc.

We acknowledge the support of The Canada Council for the Arts and the Manitoba Arts Council for our publishing program.

Acknowledgements
Versions of some of these poems appeared in *Jones Av* magazine, *The Wayward Coast: Anthology 2004* and this writer's *The Last Trip to Oregon* (Ronsdale Press: Vancouver, 2002). *Alterations* is pervasively informed by the work of other artists, notably the composers Ludwig van Beethoven and Johann Sebastian Bach, the painter J.M.W. Turner, saxophonist Jan Garbarek, and many writers, especially Wallace Stevens and Theodore Roethke. The endnotes provide further detail. More immediately, this book owes its existence to the village of Roberts Creek – a place, a people, a state of mind. Like Bunny Wright's Sechelt, it is an actual place on the Sunshine Coast of British Columbia, mildly fictionalized in these pages. Some of its people bear their own names here, to their apparent pleasure. My special thanks to Joe Dougherty, of Joe Road, an old friend who claims he moved here because it was the only place he could find an address under his own cognomen. Joe gave these poems insightful thought and nourishment as though they were his own. John John Morris, exemplary man, exemplary friend, sustains me as he does many others. Tony Barrett, classicist at the University of British Columbia, straightened out my οἶνοψ for me. *Namaste* to Mark Boyter – writer, photographer, traveller. And my of course abiding gratitude to George "Shamble" Amabile, who edited with rambling discernment, an acute ear, and great strength – as he does everything.

Library and Archives Canada Cataloguing in Publication

Payerle, George, 1945–
Alterations / George Payerle

ISBN 0-921833-97-0

I. Title.

PS8581.A847A84 2004 C811'.54 C2004-906005-8

Signature Editions, P.O. Box 206, RPO Corydon, Winnipeg, Manitoba, R3M 3S7

For Phyllis & Bronwen

and the family of Amy Dundas

as though god had said
    I am patience   I am space   I am
nothing
        substantial
as the voices infolded into multifoliate flame
    Old Ludwig heard
when he heard the silence.

TABLE OF CONTENTS

ALTERATIONS

FINAL THINGS

ENDNOTES

CEDAR GROVE

For Dr Russ, Sarah D, Marcel & Imnaha

COASTING

They came in grace,
    angels of the paradigm
strolling madrona beaches of Davis Bay
                    soft steel unto the blue bones
of the Island.

This place gives god –
grace of cedar, fir, salal and weeds
    antiparadigm anaparadigm –
a thought containing our absence
    into which we make incursion
like Israeli armour into Palestinian dust.

It is among the rocks we have placed our mattresses,
slept with swordfern
and pale copper-green skin of madrona;
Joni Mitchell lives here
yet we are paving paradise.

We become accustomed to
serenity
    Roberts Creek Wilson Creek Sechelt
    Gibsons
accustomed to our rural polity
until three kids in baseball caps
and a broken-down logger wearing shades
seem cool and cynical
as the civic millions.

Daft and hopeless as rain,
the coho flashing silver sunbursts
to leaven with light
the graceful waters of Davis Bay.

Mustagh Tower

A mountain of the Karakoram –
last blue mountain barred with snow:
In Roberts Creek today
a man named Mike bred to snow and wolves
sold me the moosehorn Earth Goddess
he'd carved –
around my neck, *namaste* from
the cedar grove I live in,
heavy-butted steatopyga
with huge pendulous breasts
                                        touching
her Buddha-navel,
my own
and Mike's hard-bitten pseudo-hippy
trapline soul
in this evanescent time
I can momently afford
and never repay,
like that last blue mountain
that's killed more than climbed it
because it's there.

Br. 219 RCL

Dusty green leaves of something I cannot name
surround a lamppost in the Legion parking lot:
Roberts Creek.
The neighbour's white floribunda cascade over the fence –
an improbability,
English cottage gone to seed,
garden of our recent hundred-year antiquity
here far colonized
and Coast as ever blackfish
and the rocky coves of longing all up and down
this gunkholed wetside paradise.

1167 Cedar Grove

There are many stations in this house
large
amongst its sunlight cedars:
peace
space
places
to be,
my study outdoors
a toolshed nirvana
and
and
I can get lost here in .42 acres
of pure amazement
where in my own house I assay
countless
studies of being
home.

10 SEPTEMBER, ROBERTS CREEK

Looking at the Milky Way. Yeh.
The rest of the world is my neighbours,
cedar, fir and balsam.

There were two old guys
leaning on the bridge in Harbertonford
a couple of lifetimes ago. One spat,
the other sucked a pipe.
They spoke once in a while,
briefly, and
looked at the little river rushing by
under their feet,
until the green bus came along from Moreleigh,
stopped, and went on again to Harberton,
which is a barnyard,
leaving them to do what they did
each afternoon:
mind the unfolding of the universe.

This afternoon, two old guys played Scrabble
on my deck in Roberts Creek.
One of them was me.

THE MONTH AFTER 11 SEPTEMBER

A ship, an isle, a sickle moon –
With few but with how splendid stars
The mirrors of the sea are strewn
Between her silver bars.†

No sea.
A wave of dark firs rises
against the black pellucid sky
Orion and all stars scattered
through ghostlight of the crescent moon –
Pleiades' green-haze glittering eyes

Stratospheric whistle overhead,
    navlights of a jetliner arrow NW → SE
and one thinks, "commercial, civilian,
                                        safe –"
and one is wrong.

Di's deck, Salt Spring Island
11 October 2001

† James Elroy Flecker

NEBULAE

What is sufficient?
The brawling monologue
of a dipso hoper
willing to waste my time and talent
on his story:
broken bones of a life at sea,
in government, and bars.

What drunkards
have I known in all these places
so alike
never two the same.
What drunkards have I dreamed
Buddhists in pursuit of icons
and sufficiency.

There is a slowness in the universe
into which we pool
and draw those others
bewildered into stillness.

The mirror sees itself,
glass,
emptiness,
infinity,
eternal now
companionable
as the "I" of god.

The Iron Rabbit

Bix and the iron rabbit
guard the door –
the iron rabbit by assignment
(doorstop, hearthrabbit, folk art, icon),
Bix by choice. Temple cat. Ancient
(105 in human years). Icon.
Varied job descriptions for two beasts,
the one more or less immortal,
the other an ageless incarnation
with the voice of Beiderbecke's cornet,
though tuneless,
that sleeps serenely in my armpit
each long and blessed night.

SUMMER RAIN

reminds us that it's possible to die,
cool air,
moist precipitate, fresh
as dispassionate thought
and that elegant figuration of Benn's –
        Worst of all:
        not to die in summer,
        when everything is bright,
        and the earth is easy on the spade
– three years before his death
after seventy years of numinous pessimism
that saw gentleness
at the heart of all brutal grotesqueries
our flesh endures
before its final corruption,
as here might be
under this delicate wet patter
prescient of autumn's unleaving,
winter's decay
and the gleam of eternal light.

General Store

Toing and froing each day once at least
from Cedar Grove along Beach to Walter's store,
Cathy's Post Office, the little library
or Joe's Gumboot Café,
I walk a small-purposed constitutional past homes
of friends and neighbours whose lives
repeat themselves like mine
expecting little more or less than the everything
this Coast provides
under the varying skies of Roberts Creek
in our cyclic journeying
from bright child wonder
to Lethe's shadowed shore.

IT'S NOT ENOUGH

to begin or cease.
Nothing is but going makes it so –
to leave to stay,
to return to go

EROTIC ACHRONOMETRIC

for George Amabile

The night time, the sweet time,
the neither waking nor sleeping time,
the slow erogeny
at any time of day,
real as bricks and bones,
different utterly from the day time, "real time,"
think and do and act time,
this erodreamtime
pretending only to be all time,
this time
every time.

From Gower Point to Irvines Landing

The men with bulldozers in their eyes
have mostly gone on pogey now, or into rest homes
or the grave
Mad Frenchy ran
the Gulf Oil in Madeira Park,
Maudzi Anglais! to any customer who looked sideways
at anything
or got in his cuestick's way on the plywood floors up
the Rigger's Roost looking over Garden Bay;
fell in love with him, or him with me
across the butt-end of that pool cue one hot day
thirty-two summers ago, when everyone figured me
for a cityslick Summer boy with his hippychick,
and I smiled into Frenchy's deadly sea-blue eyes and
we ended up drinking Blue out of bottles down in the
bent-chrome midden he called home, out back the Gulf,
Tombstones in his eyes   And after that
he'd phone and say "Where ya been, white boy?"
and we'd pound down unmixed boilermakers sweating in the sun
while he tried to egg me into fistfights
over T.S. Eliot vs Jules Laforgue or which end is up
when you've been down so long   End up in rassling matches
in the dust, him small and strong as a terrier's jaws, me long and sneaky,
lying flat on our backs drunk as skunks staring at the cerulean sky,
"The underbelly of God, white boy, the underbelly of God"
Gone, somewhere,
with all his less agreeable friends and foes
who ruled this coast with chainsaws and peavies and
fists quicker'n sledgehammers
We miss them God knows we miss them,
though there never was a damn thing you could do,
except beer for beer, shot for shot, a poem for a punch
in the head

Glad the old Pen Hotel's gone, where the only
way not to eat a pool cue was feed one to the other guy
first, or run   No good, the Pen   But I miss
old Gilles Lalonde and the Rigger's plywood floor gone
cutesy Hallmark pink and mauve,
those lean and hungry scruff-faced bastards

who decided I wasn't what I seemed, though I was,
once Frenchy took me under his steel-belted wing
The way I think sometimes
the lonely forests miss
those guys come humping block and tackle up the sidehill
to clearcut the mothers down

Thirty years ago and more,
already this Coast was dying,
though no one would've been left standing
had it lived on   And I'm still waiting on a postcard
from Frenchy to say the beer's fine and the women finer
there where the dead poets dance
on the other side of the hill

The little islands

sail gilt and bluestone waters
off Secret Cove and Trail Bay and the numberless
bights and bays and covelets kinking this coast
like intestinal convolutions,
little islands like afterthoughts of god,
but that big one, that dark, snow-topped, sawtooth
behemoth blocking horizon to horizon for four hundred miles,
that continental breakwater
that makes this south coast paradise,
that's a definite part of the divine Sitkan plan,
inside water from Juan de Fuca to Scott Point
which we're now turning into an urban shit tank.

Old Stump

Way out in the backyard at the new forest's edge,
eight-foot high and punk-rotten,
it grows young cedars thick as Catriona Le May Doan's lovely thighs
and clean-sawn then made a table you could eat from
or stand on and move the world,
as it was then,
                              movable,
they said.
And so it seemed,
when speedskaters ran the steel-hard rivers east of here
naked under god's eye
brushing cedar fronds from his gaze.

Bix Baking in July

Old cat beached on the back deck like a thin little furry whale
raises his head, squints sunken rheumy eyes against the glare
and brevity of life before him.
His sidekick and alpha-dominant compadre went under the bricks
at the ides of January   Buried him, my spotty dotty silver-charcoal pal
with sprigs of winter oregano and cedar boughs
under the gritty till of Cedar Grove, narrow rectangle of glacial rock
to mark his length and breadth, dead stick for headstone, he
who had started the armpit-sleeping trick his buddy emulated
and so if I slept alone I slept with a beast tucked either side, snoring heads
laid high on the round of my shoulder bones and the night he lay dying
on the hallway oak I lay down by him and he curled-in that same old way,
my friend Maui, cat not island, who spoke mostly when spoken to,
squeaked like a rusted hinge, charged like a bull, ran catlife including Bix's,
when they were young, for a block around. Strange tom came in the yard,
they'd hunt him as a pair, Maui charging spotted black-silver streak to hit
a little feline ton, when green-brown mackerel Bix had circled to helicopter in
from four feet high, twenty claws hooked to rake. Quick toms fled. Slow toms
got bowled and slashed for a bale of catwool and shrieking. Bix howled like
a hound when I placed the stones on Maui's grave. Oriental shorthairs,
but the one Abyssinian in his heart and bones wrapping around my shoulders
like a silver stole; the other a Siamese Egyptian born to temple cat his life away
contemplating the mystery. He's now within months of the age when Maui
went, withering though eating six meals a day, horking too many all over the
rugs (in a house mostly oak and maple floored), eyes sinking into his geriatric
consciousness, bones staggering with arthritis,
but going out to charge the neighbour toms since the Maui marines are gone,
and his own helicopter days done
and he's king cat now; no waiting for death,
baking in the sunblasted backdeck heat, gone already
to the feline paradise so like the cooler regions of hell
with clear skies, birds and cedar trees.

The Black Current

Acolytes of dissolution,
we are surrounded by broken marriages,
absent friends, jobless friends, a dying cat,
and if the sun don't shine this August
we'll know el niño and la niña are in bed again
making hemispheric incest
to emulate their relatives Atlantic-side,
saying, Call the kettle black, motherfuckers,
yer hothouse gases
and acid rain and ef flu ent
fuck yu.

Turneresque: Sketches of the Divine

Garbarek of a grey noon in August,
chants gregorian in mode from time ago
when sanctity and the plague walked abroad by day
beneath a clear alto line sailing heavenward,
the soul of prayer,
joyous pathos of despair and hope
Rodin captured in his *Burghers of Calais,*
and Miles Davis in Spain
when jazz was a whole lot younger,
Casals still alive to make Bach's sonorities ring
under the austere Catalan sky,
and Jan Garbarek being born Norwegian
to learn the mystic's voice
in a bent brass horn,
plainsong sombre and shining with god's light,
a trick of the weather to incandesce this vapid
sky to a Turneresque
beyond us as we are
the cedars glowing green as creation,
this luminous faith incarnate
to suffuse all who endure
mere mortality.

BEACH AVENUE

21 August

for Chris & Kathryn Vile, of Gooseford

Forest light at dusk turns
rose among the scented trees,
brightening cedar green and cedar brown,
softening line,
as the tors of Dartmoor shine
above those blurred rose-purple slopes
revisited so long ago
and now in album photos
of touring fair Devonians,
their golden children,
as well as in the mind
now turning 57
along this rough Pacific shore
while rose and softening light
deepens the shadows
of this warmly growing night,

the view from a wet red-mud crest
along the road from Rolster Bridge,
near Harbertonford,
where Roman legions marched
toward the sea
from their camp on the hill of Totnes:

rose-purple furze and granite tors
unconquered these millennia,
this blood-red Devon of the soul.

Beach Avenue

They are things chalked
On the sidewalk so that the pensive man may see.
– Wallace Stevens

And as it passes by, I have
no time to worry
when the moment will come, as
it's all about
whenever
I go walking down the avenue
of forest and homes, BMWs & junkers
shacks & mansions
and the sea,
they're all here,
grannies & mums and wee to mid-size,
gangling tall or hipster curvy blonde
progeny,
dads and other guys,
axe-thwack and chainsaw roar,
the wound-up hornet whine
cutting & trimming & splitting
and planing and honing
and toting their tots on their shoulders,
dogs and kids ambulatory
in either or all hands
running
along the twists & straights & slopes
of Beach Avenue.

The high eagle soars,
the Strait of Georgia slaps and thumps
the shingle shore,
the sunbeaten sea glinting brass
some Achaean armourer might have forged
for the plains of Troy
and Nanaimo wonders it can seem so far away
below that hulking Forbidden Plateau.

The high eagle claims us,
flesh-bearing ants
            in the intricate nest he sees.
And the pensive man claims the eagle
hunting along Beach Avenue.

An Anabasis

Devil's club and salal
pour down the deadfall-tangled valleys
and lead us, lost, thrashing & spine-pricked
to the sea,
    thalassa   thalassa,
where no Coaster can be lost
any more than the Greeks
wise Xenophon led and followed
    home.

PREECE,

who lives next door,
was once a Birmingham girl,
went on to be a dancer
in Babylon by the Bay,
married a man who didn't work out
but brought her to Roberts Creek.
Now she sits at August's sunset
by the mandala near the pier
down-handy Beach and the General Store
as the folk unwind in stupor
from the Creek Daze
she makes happen every year,
the festival and carnival and love-in
born of Fall Fair custom
this quarter century ago,
and it might as well be Preece Days now,
Creekers drifting by her in their scores
to say How ya doin' Sarah
now your yearly chore is done?
Just fine, she says, but tired
(smiling), and a little felted in the brain.

She's straggle-haired and wan-faced now
in sloppies for the beach,
this Sunday by the sea –
was Morgan le Fay of the Friday Ball,
slim hourglass black-gowned
with empress curls jet
at her clear patrician brow,
snowy bosom she somehow magicked
from a shape mostly Peter Pan,
an Audrey Hepburn femme fatale,
semi-tragic heroine
ethereal in the jam-packed hall.

The sun goes down on Georgia Strait
and the mouth of Roberts Creek,
the Creekers sprawled all happy,
hung over and trying to eat
the fixin's they brought down
for Sarah and her Creek Daze crew –

'most everyone you meet.
The sun goes down on Sarah's eyes
so tired they can hardly see,
yet shining still with the inner light
that sparks their darkness live and
crinkly as pearls of sheer obsidian,
surveying the people, who have made
this dogeared rural paradise their home
and the twilight and the bonfires and
the music and the children
make it seem like the Mira at Marion Bridge
of an evening on that older maritime shore
four thousand miles away,
while Sarah drifts in dreams of
what's right here before her and the Daze
she's seen to bed,
drifts on to dreamland waiting
when she's utterly not awake,
yet planning Daze to come
all dancing in her head
as the fire that fuels the light
still shines within her eyes,
the fire that makes her Preece.

WRITING, ON

These days

begin before autumn dawn
like wolves bright wakened
        and plunging through darkness
with the joy of birds
that sing among the cedar tops
        all the stars
and a fiercely waning moon.

These wolves,
        icey eyed,
lunge toward humankind east of sunrise,
jaws parted to snap and tear and pull lives down,
this rush of lean, sable-furred spirit things
encircling, darting, seizing blood-jewelled prey
for their many-mouthed hunger,
dancing choreography of a single mind,
tribal will of the moonlit pack
with fangs innumerable as the half-seen stars,
these wolves, these days,
herding prey toward consummation
innocent yet as ewes
with lamb.

Glenn Plays Diana

Krall's lovely eyes watch
from a paper folded so nose and chin
don't spoil the picture,
watch Gould strike the opening bars
of the Italian Concerto, starsparks
scattered precise and hot to awaken
the black velvet sky of all music
she gazes upon in awed repose,
temptress struck dumb
                    in her newsprint world
by this brighter light pinpricking
torchlit tunes, priapic Chryslers
she glosses with that svelte shape
and prognathous jaw,
moon-huntress singing covers
of other people's songs,
this Nanaimo bar girl
played in her dream
by the stark angel
of Johann Sebastian's
                    polyphonic theology,
who lately serenaded giraffes
at the Toronto zoo.

THOREAU

I have this Walden towel,
moss-green, striated white,
calm woodland pool
in the washroom Martha Stewart forgot,
balm for welcome infrequent guests
and me:

I drove once as passenger by your pond,
Henry David,
of a chill morning in New England August
and saw a boat I might have imagined
the man in it an implication
of darkened mist
as though nothing had changed
and now I tread dewy December grass,
persistent dandelions still yellow
after frost
and speak with the two spiders
womanning tattered webs
in the lamp-warmed space
among the stacks of my backwood shed
that stores books by everyone, including you,
till libraries can be built under these cedars
who breathe the air
you warmed with wintry, workboot
contemplation.

Garbage

after Joe Dougherty

First you have to put it in the bag,
after remembering to put the paper
and the cardboard
and the shiny paper
and the brown paper bags
but not the brown envelopes
and the plastic numbered 1, 2, & 4
but not the plastic numbered 3, 5, or 6
or any other plastic
and the clean steel tins and the clean
aluminum tins
and the respective lids of each
and the refund-bearing bottles and
cartons but not the milk cartons
whether of cows or soy beans
and not the lids of plastic bottles
no matter what their number
and the newspapers
                    the newspapers
                              the newspapers
(have we read the newspapers?)
to say nothing of magazines
and oh yes the non-refundable glass bottles
jars and other glass of different colours sometimes
into separate receptacles
and then you have to remember the garbage
and the garbage in the other garbage receptacles
and remember when it's Thursday
and remember to put the garbage out
and not let the coons and dogs get in it
and then the truck comes before you remember
to do all that
                  and if necessary you run after the truck
hopefully, waving
and the guy is always happy to have one more bag
and it goes away
never to be seen again,
we think.

Only Morning

No wolves these days:
only morning hours before the sun
as the dark grows shorter
millimetre by millimetre now
the Solstice has been burned
in the forests of Roberts Creek.
These ashen days
slink wet and bedraggled,
demoralized dogs
that rolled in the stinking blubber
another seal has left to rot among the seawrack –
this Coast
    this Coast
hunched into global-warming winter
as a new rough beast staggers toward Bethlehem
to be born sometime after the dim epiphany
in mundo cane this coarse American Bush
broods upon
while the dead seals bark and sing
sad threnodies
at the decay of apocalypse into apoplexy
in dismal pre-dawn light.

Christmas 2002

after Jim Scott by telephone

Allelujah Allelujah the CBC sings Handel,
bless it. Christmas rains greyly among all these
things so always green, perennial Christmas greens
that make "Christmas greens" irrelevant
now as always in this perennially herbaceous celebration
lit by strings of coloured lamps and raindrops scattered
starbright among all the catkins and twisty branches of hazel *contorta*
right there –
all, all shining
and it is good   and earlier CBC replayed the end of 1938
looking forward to the promise of 1939
and I wonder here among the cedar trees of Roberts Creek
what unseasonable darkness broods
                                        at the heart of our Mother Corporation,
considering the promise of 2003 in its hourly news
that the end of world is nigh,
as it was by September 1939,
we at the eve of what Holocaust now?
What Stalingrad and Leningrad and Blitz
and Nanking and Hiroshima and Nagasaki
to pale the Bosnias and Rwandas
our placid souls lament as horrors safely far
as last week's garbage on the dump.
When was it we first heard of the truth? *The the.*
Allelujah.

Praise Ye the Lord

Handel knew as few have done
that joy is surprise
and celebration, joy:
ALLELUJAH! ZADOC THE PRIEST!
which gave the English the only anthem
which surprises, if only they'd sing it right
as Malcolm Sargent made the Royal Philharmonic do
to bounce a Vancouver audience out of its seats
as though brass and tympani were the Allelujah Chorus
and Johann Sebastian's B-Minor Gloria always does
and the English always are surprising, from one
annus horribilis to another, poor Queen,
of Divine Right to rule not a thing,
not Commonwealth nor family nor the Grim Reaper,
and humour is surprise,
why Handel and Bach make one laugh
while weeping,
as joy does,
the tinge of mortality in human celebration,
the whimsy
at the heart of divinity.
They say aboriginals laugh all the time –
a fuller understanding of god
given as the sun popping out of the horizon
at the wrong time of day
by German composers, a very long time ago.
The Haida word for Raven.
The hilarity of invention.
The discovery of fire,
touched by an innocent hand.

Dogs Euthanized after Savaging Shenica

Pace. The beasts have run enough,
devoured enough, havocked enough,
deranged with sweat and exhaustion. *Pace.*
Shoot them if you must. The peace of many.
Lead, kindly light – *Dominus vobiscum* – for thou art a dog
and may thy hide at least be tanned
to keep some poor yobbo from freezing in the rain,
but understand that they are bewildered and lost,
children strayed too far in play when the sun goes down,
no more, or less, evil than the rock that falls
from the mountain, the tree blown down.
None of this would matter if we weren't here,
and chaos could run a different course
untrammelled by *homo sapiens* .

Gumboot Nation

for Their Majesties Doug & Helen

Doug Roy stumps down along his shore,
knees just barely fit for duty
winter and summer while the sea prowls the rock
and shingle around his boots. He is
King of the Gumboot Nation,
wintry eyes searching out the ghost of Hubert Evans
in the mist on the river at the mouth of Roberts Creek.
Doug squints and says, "We've met. Do I know you?"
holds out a bearlike paw. "Yes, last summer
at the Creek Daze, when you read your grandson's piece."
Clenches my hand in an iron grip. "Ah yes,
my grandson Ben. Writes well for a city whelp."
Squints hard and says, "Thought I'd seen you. Never
know anymore with these eyes."
These eyes see through me to old Hubert
pulling stumps with a team of mules
and young Ben Stoller strolling Omaha Avenue
on Algonquin Island at the civic edge of Lake Ontario,
an ice cream in his hand. The wind blows up from Georgia Strait,
lashes spindrift 'round our ears. "We've met," Doug Roy repeats,
clear growl like the seawash gravel at our feet."Who are you?"
"A scribe," I yell into the wind, "a friend."
"Good!" giving my hand a final crunch, "that's good." His eyes
crinkle like sunlight on ice. "Need friends, these days. These
city folks ..." And stumps off along his shore, his Queen Helen
plucking kelp for pickles from the shallows among the rocks
far down the misty, spume-sheeted beach. I think of Hubert Evans,
hunched over tea in his kitchen twenty years ago,
looking like Henry Moore at the time he was drawing sheep
and hedgerows back home in Yorkshire,
sheep and hedgerows all alike in gnarled black lines full of light.
Roberts himself, Evans and Roy and Paul Czernevsky:
These brawny, long-thewed men who carved a human village
from the cedar and fir and rock we're now threatening
with suburban malls and clearcut housing estates.
The sea curls cold through gutta percha around my ankles,
and I can't see a thing in the billowing scud.
The King and Queen of the Gumboot Nation, somewhere
in the chiaroscuro of this shadow weather, first and last
monarchs of the Quingdom of Roberts Creek,

fade into the everfreshening mists.
I hear seas beginning to crash, a luminous line offshore,
thunder of the moments rolling into billows smashed
on the wreckage of a time-despoiled coast. The forest groans.
In its grinding tangle a fir scorned as timber snaps
and takes the power grid with it. The computer screens
blink dark as the houses and I'm blown off the beach
like seawrack slipping among stones and driftwood
toward a low-tech fire and cats twining around
my legs for company as much as feed. But the men in hardhats
and slickers and rubber-soled boots will come by here
to turn it all back on again.
That's good. But in the firelight and shadow weather
and sheets of cedar water pouring astringent from the trees,
it's easier to see what Doug Roy sees
through those age-dimmed eyes like winter glass.

ALTERATIONS

Orion's Horse

The stars are brightly shining.
No wolves, these days
in the barely frozen pre-dawn night:
Horses. Presence of horses unseen
in the darker forest,
the whole sky a black stallion's hide
bestrid by tall Orion,
followed by his dog,
all stars beads of celestial sweat
on the fields of honour beyond us
as we see a blind man stagger toward the sea,
τὸν οἴνοπα πόντον, the wine dark sea
restless as blood
and aim his cane
like a rifle
and the black hole at its muzzle's end.

The News

Since that eleventh of September
we listen.
Perhaps it will happen again. Perhaps
something worse,
perhaps something is always happening
to distract us from seeing those towers fall
again and again and again
the fireball of dead pilots and screaming passengers
and projectile vomit jet fuel burning steel
full of humanity falling
incalculably as *Challenger's* seven astronauts
in their own brief meteor-star.

TRACES: THE NEW YEAR 2003

Preece's smoke blows down the road,
banked fire to remind me
of winter's slow burn –
how long this old Circean technology
can last against clean-air rhetoric
and the busy bug-noise circuitry
chittering away like termites in her brain
as the Peter Pan magician hides her mirrors
in the smoke lest she see age withering there
as certain as modernity
and less easily fooled.

These incinerated traces of the past,
bucked and split boles of trees
fifty or sixty years old,
portend a new year greyly shadowed
by dense particulate clouds of human
garbage burning in the firepits we'll call
history: Pyongyang, Baghdad,
Chechnya, Palestine … Palestine …
George Bush mounting global firestorms
while the Pope makes vague arthritic
fiddle noises in Rome.

The Immaculate Weight of Being

Sys Schau's shoulder
in faded purple terrycloth robe,
Phyllis Surges leaning her weight upon me
as the horses do,
our daughter at the far end of a tack trunk
strong as a man,
my father's body
lightened by his spirit's flight,
Di Hayes' heart leaden with grief
a gift of trust in healing,
Red Lillard's ashes evanescent as air,
my mother in a wheelchair
staring at the nullity slowly
replacing her life like the silicates
which become a fossilized fern.
These moments before life –
the conception of star seed,
the nebulae before and after creation,
the final unendable poem of being,
the white dwarf at the edge of perception,
the absence and presence of light,
the specific gravity of the soul.

The Axle of History

The old brown hen and the old blue sky,
Between the two we live and die –
The broken cartwheel on the hill.
– *Wallace Stevens*

We live at the still point
between Gower Point and Irvines Landing
where the last sawmill closed last year
and the fishing fleets are crowded
from the yacht basins. The wheel has broken
as the cart went by.

A log-skidder's arch stands off the highway
like the pelvic girdle of a stegosaur,
and just as relevant bearing the name
of the man who lives there; prompts the question
"What's that?" as the SUVs trundle by.
Gatepost to a world gone as the dodo bird.

Time was, the Wheelwright of Akenfield
lived down the road, stopped at the pub,
bespoke the painted waggons of his youth
that rolled into the last dusty harvest
before his father died, gave his name as Jubal
Merton, aged sixty, who'd never been away.

Time was, the man who felled
the old-growth giant in my back yard
lived next door; but that was before
my time writing in this shack the old horse-
logger's neighbour built as workshop toolshed
and the joists are rotting out.

Time was, Red and I could test-drive
an old Sointula double-ender, him a bush Alaskan
at the helm, who'd piloted his teenhood skiff
out Clover Passage looking for Rilke somewhere
on the way to Wrangell, loving this Chrysler
Crown six-banger as he clipped through the chop

in the civil waters off Oak Bay, trailing an entire
Sitkan coast of ghosts in salmon light
I can only wave goodbye to, like old Frenchy Lalonde
and big Doug Roy I'm only meeting as he stumps
away into the rainshadows of this Coast
I was born into and arrive at too late.

The mist of morning fills with memory
shared among the cedar trees and salal working
to reclaim our lawns. Vegetal memory old as the
blood suffusing Devon mud. Yellow JCB backhoe
sits nose to nose with Phyllis's yellow Focus coupe
it could hoist in its clam-bucket jaw

before Bill Wells restratifies our garden
to her vision of planted berms, drystream boulders …
a copper oak, coral-bark maple, red-twig dogwood
and ceanothus blue eyes winking in the dawn.
In a thousand years, if printed words exist,
they'll read of us, and some human geographer

will trace the workings of Bill Wells and all the
backhoe operators, concrete pourers and boulder merchants,
sniff out the politics and pettifoggeries of our paleskin
tribes among the aboriginal forests, and see perhaps
the colour of our blood anciently staining this sandy
yellow glacial till full of more rocks than sense.

By then it'll make no matter that oyster gatherers
and slave-club makers, timber fallers and backhoe men
no longer rub elbows with each other and all the computer
hacks have been subsumed in the microest chip an aeon
since the last wheelwright was gone from contemplation
of the broken cartwheel and our axle's turning.

This time is different, our time, not our fathers' time:
Scott died in the Antarctic when my dad was three;
claimed he saw Halley's Comet at age one. Now
Columbia's crew falling like chaff at mach 18 defines
our past – yesterday – *Challenger* in '86 – the towers
fall, forever, and America bedevils the world

as no nation could before. Halley came by again
when I was forty; saw a patch of haze out there by night.
Next time, my daughter would be 81. That comet now
the only thing we can count on. Jubal Merton said,
*The body-work was all painted blue. Always blue. The blue
rode well in the corn,* in Akenfield not so long ago.

Now and then

in memoriam Jon Furberg, 1944–92

we wonder, when
the sun comes up
or doesn't,
if it matters;
and the daughter
of one's middle 30s
is the daughter of one's later 50s,
near the age her mother was
when we first met.

And then I think of Furberg –
"what came next came then,
after that" – the man who wrote *Prepositions,*
"and we kept talking and drinking,
then it finished right after that
and he passed the hat
and that was that."

Now it's twenty years since then
and he lived ten more
and then I wore red shoes when he died
and now is still now, as it was then
when Bronwen was two or three and thirteen
and Furberg a man far larger than what he did,
both before and after
warm fingers could no longer twine
in his hair so curling fine.

And now prospect is becoming retrospect
and after that we wonder,
now and then,
and then they'll wonder now
what was before
and what comes after,
now, and then:
so now and then becomes we and they,
and now is always now,
until then.

Paxil and I: Thoughts of Roethke & Woolf

Six hours a day I lay me down
Within this tub but cannot drown.
– *Theodore Roethke*

Ted, you meditated in hydrotherapy
and while I don't know yet
if you died by water or fire or the noose,
the ice cap at your rigid neck did not, at last,
keep you with the quick.
I do not laugh; I do not cry;
I'm sweating out the will to die.
Alas that thick cabbagy body
held sweat enough for many deaths,
but you loved a trashed geranium
and found sad triumph of your will.

Tried pills myself, hypnotic allure
of sleeping forever sooner than ordained
when I couldn't sleep at all.
Did the booze not serve Morpheus at last,
but leave you shrieking at the abyss
you couldn't miss? *Who cried, in goose, Alas?*
I do well with little pink tablets now,
mournful at worst when the demons
step up the stair
their basilisk eyes and Medusa hair
confounded by mere sorrow.

I miss you, Ted, cantankerous buckaroo of greenhouses
I probably wouldn't have liked; and you're better off
gone sooner than ordained by infirmity; but here I sit,
paxilled beyond immediate despair,
listening to Garbarek pipe up the dawn
in plaintive cries of loons and wind and sea,
:rarum ii the collation of his life's voices
reed brass wild and high as anything you wrote,
the pure serene of memory in one man
in a far field wide as the world; I'd rather you were here,
a bottle of whisky, Phyllis's geraniums red as blood

so we could both go down to sit in the River Ouse
with rocks in our pockets and contemplate infinity
alongside sad Virginia, whose father called her Jinny,
knowing as little of who she was as yours when he swung
you high above the rosebeds among his glasshouse walls,
not drowning, but being. Virginia, no Kraut you, but god
knows what might have been, had you soaked your fine
smeddum gentility in company with that German peasant
and this preserved Hungarian enduring time since they made
little pills more skookum than the talking cure, sleeping draughts
or the purblind tortures of a less human hydrotherapy.

PHARISEES 1:1

And so it was that the dead went before them
and they cried "Let us commemorate the dead"
and raised memorials to those gone before them
and went in the march of time to kill others.
Rivet me to the sky, Lord, rivet me to the sky.
Percy Bysshe fell upon the thorns of life, Lord.
Rivet me to the sky.

The C-Word as Redemption

I can't do *cunt* the justice Sharon Olds does,
not only because I haven't one:
after all, her "Pope's Penis" is
as fine a covert dangling clapper
as any man could hope for.
But *vulva in situ*
is sweet-scented redemption for a culture
in dread of the sacred, whether it be
the ineffable soul, or its organs of generation
carried crucially between the legs. As Willy
Yeats declared, *Love has pitched his mansion in
The place of excrement* .... And we not only
avert our face from the fact Christ had balls,
we fail to consider His toilet arrangements,
long days handing out loaves and fishes to
multitudes who must have pissed a lot and
shat somewhere.

I asked a woman lovely in her bones
what she thought of *cunt* the word, and she
said, "It's the right word, but I can't speak it
without blushing," unblushingly naked in
conversation neither pre nor post coital. "*Cock*'s
different," perhaps because she hasn't one,
a woman female in her bones and fond
of *penis erectus* and *testes dependens*
whether direct or indirect.

"*Suckhole* shouldn't be derogatory!" another
woman snapped. "I treasure having my hole
sucked. It's sacred." Amazing me, since I'd
never thought that term more gender specific
than *kiss my ass*. And when a mother showed
me a photo of her naked daughter and said,
"Why should she be ashamed of her hole? I
have one too!" I murmured "*Cunt*'s a better
word ..." "But it's obscene!"

Infolded in dusky quiet or opened to
a garnet-ringed O, delicate labia minora
translucent to a candle-flame they puff out
with one sharp contraction, hushed pagan moment
sacred as transubstantiation of water into wine,
light of the spirit into incandescent flesh
through which all human life is borne,
serene ἔκστασις in a cradle of bone.

MILLING

Winds to 90 kilometres an hour
sunshine and showers

Threads of gangue unwind from the mind
bright rococo decoration
for a dim and cluttered inscape
as the poet becomes a pipefitter,
the golden bird a figment, byzantine cabal,
a glitter beyond the mind's turning
as the pipes leak liquids and gases
and the vision becomes mop-strokes
on a sodden floor, awaiting chance
explosions; the presence of god
a tangled toolbox, lost wrenches.
The sky polishes itself.
The widowmakers sway.
The fingers stray over brittle strands
that curl like fried hair and prick skin
with a bright dusting of blood.

Sky: A Clearing in Cedar Grove

for Al & Sue Clyde

The brightness of the sky
is bigger now
since Phyllis condemned the seven cedars
and Sue and Al across the road carved
the Valley of Clyde from the forest
they inhabit. I would a sky
big as Saskatchewan, freezing my fingers
outside the Whitewood café on a smokebreak
while the Greyhound rests,
talking with a Manitoba farmer
in the clearing between the grain elevator
and the trees around the first house at Indian Head
about the best land in Canada – except maybe
down by Carman where I went once
with Amabile to buy roses that never could
outwinter Winnipeg. I would a sky
big as the chinook arch over pronghorns
amber in winter grassland,
the Greyhound stretching out for Brooks
from Lethbridge just before the sun bit the Rockies.
I would a sky big as the night, westing from Brandon,
when the full moon last November lit a prairie
you could touch forever
in every twig and grassblade and silvered undulation
before your fingers froze off
and you staggered into Swift Current at the hour of the wolf.
I would such a sky,
but miss the seven heavy boles
gracing my front yard with endless conversation
before Tom Stanway took them down.

Testes Dei Ridentis

That a man should grow a third testicle
at age 57, pseudo though it be,
makes sad comment on age and sense. As a
woman said long ago, elbows are
absurd
and the body may well be
the worst joke God came up with,
were it not for the mind.

That a man should have balls
is truism and tautology:
to kill a lion to become a man,
lionlike. To eat my enemy's testicles.
They tell me I have an intrascrotal cyst,
like a woman's ovarian,
although the tubal analogy seems
less than parallel.

These things in their rough furry sac –
ovoid, rubbery, thermally motile –
have seldom seemed more than
inconvenient, an occasionally
desirable vulnerability
with the miraculous power
to spark life
in ecstasy of incarnation.

DOLOURS

To look at the news, the weather, the *e*-
con-o-mi, we have dolours
the way in my youth we had
constant throbbing pain and
took Anacin for nagging relief.
The King Billies and Kaiser Bills and
Bomber Harrises, General LeMays,
Marshal Zhukovs all threw bomb-balls in,
as Willy Yeats had it in the widening gyre,
but now George W. has lost his falcons
in the desert,
and looks to end like Gordon at Khartoum.

Child

I'm a five-year-old now
in the world that began
when Red died.
Strange thought,
and stranger still
that my daughter's a year younger
than her mother when I met her,
and that we get younger as we
grow older, until the last one
standing will be newborn,
as my mother was,
curled softly into her death.

Forest Gubbinal

Open the blossoms, unfurl the leaves
unharness the roads, unleash the birds
fly up, voices, in this bonfire of light,
to heel the dogs and cry out, cry out
the night has closed up shop
and gathered round as a sky-reaching crowd
of dark cedars and firs. Austere Eumenides.
We have heard you. We have heard you.
The shadow is at hand
and a hearty breakfast for the damned
giving voice
to this daily funeral pyre.

These blossoms,

these blossoms, sun-yellow washed saffron,
                                                    blood,
                                                                burgundy
among eucalyptus leaves' chalky jasper:
tulip petals fierce in pungent scent of Oz,
Queensland aridity beneath Dorothy's patent red shoes.
Moira Shearer's sorrel-bright hair
wafts a poignant colour
through this damp green swordfern air.

The ineluctable

comes for us at the dawn and evening
of any moment,
between the hailstorm and the pillow,
the gesture of the hand and the falling of the gown,
the finger on the trigger and the end of time,
the blossom of sunlight on the much-loved face,
the blossom of heart's blood on battledress,
the bird-filled shadow of the moon –
this access to the divine
tremendum dei in a petal's fall
and our final terrorized breath.

Loons Calling in Georgia Strait

for Hugh & Jeanne

Hearing the sound of Montana Lake
here at the margin of the inland sea,
I hear the cold thunk of sledge on wedge
jammed in sodden cottonwood,
the Wilsons père et fils grinning
at this soft-handed city boy
mad keen on splitting wood
while mère Jeanne smiles over pinkest gin
and fries up a London broil
as D'Oyly Carte pirates Penzance
to the counterpoint delight
of all resident loons.
Their tocsin calls make silence huge,
palpable – an ocean of space
rolling from Bridge Lake to Little Fort –
pre-dawn loons on the steely sea
from Gower Point to Arrowsmith.
Starry, starry night.
Sunstruck memory.

The Ghost of Alan Moorehead – 25 March 2003 –

ROBERTS CREEK – It's bad in that far Iraq. Armour of the 3rd Division, USA, hunkers down fifty miles short of Baghdad – about as far as Abbotsford up the Valley from Vancouver. The Desert Rats' grandsons reconsider the Basra where the ghost of an Aussie war correspondent sits in a wicker chair in the English Club, *a ramshackle single-storeyed wooden building* long forgotten since September 1941. He was in a sideshow of the North African Campaign. It was about oil. And the end of Empire – for the English. Alan Moorehead, remarkable man, would not have been an "embedded journalist" as we now use the term. But he and his colleagues embedded themselves in every major action of that campaign, and many minor ones. During the years 1940–43, Moorehead covered the course of world history from the Western Desert to Nairobi and Addis Ababa, Algeria and Tunis, Damascus, Basra, Baghdad, Teheran, and Pahlevi on the Caspian Sea, with a trip to Karachi, Delhi, Bombay and Ceylon in March of 1942. This is the time of British envoy Sir Stafford Cripps' attempt to hammer out an agreement for the independence of India. Moorehead meets with all the major players – Cripps, General Wavell, Nehru, Gandhi, Jinnah of the Muslims. But most of his time is spent covering the battles of Africa and the Middle East, often under fire, whether in the front lines or anywhere, riding whatever commandeered vehicle comes to hand in warfare as fluid as that now taking place in Iraq.

Before falling asleep on the billiard-room floor of the ramshackle building in Basra, apparently a safe rear-area in this little war, Moorehead contemplates the nature of the English clubs scattered all through the tropics. *The English Club is the place where you 'get away from the local people for a bit' … away from the shiftless squalid lives of the natives.* He goes on to foresee the *crude and tragic Hollywood thriller* in which the natives creep through the jungle and assault the club, *the sudden arrow embedded in the bar-room door,* the building going up in flames.

All this was about to happen in the Far East. One after another the English clubs were going to go up in flames–at Hong Kong and Penang, at Singapore, Rangoon and Mandalay.

In the early morning, he *woke with a jump at the sound of an explosion.* Something, as he says, was still going on. *Momentarily I half expected to see an arrow quivering in the woodwork above my head.* It had occurred to Moorehead during the night that *it might have been a better thing if the Club had been burnt down, and some of its old ideas destroyed with it. Then perhaps when we came to rebuild after the war, the native would be invited inside.*

This book, *A Year of Battle,* was first published in 1943. The most recent edition, Penguin, 2001, was published in the United States as well as the UK and Commonwealth. If you substitute *American* for *English* in the passages quoted above, Moorehead's words sound eerily contemporary. The Basra passages end thus:

You can judge the unreality of all this action in the south by the fact that throughout the fighting the Persians never cut the oil supplies. The oil flowed out of the territory held by the Persian army to the British oil refineries at Abadan and the British continued to pay their royalties. ■

Alan Moorehead died in 1983.

EACH DAY

the metal-coloured sea,
steel, lead, silver, pewter, gold
over to the crest of jagged Arrowsmith,
the whole dark ridge of Vancouver Island
the mother of all tsunamis rising.

Prodigal Daughter

A Courante for Bronwen Clea

She moves through the room,
an accidental grace
as the horses are
gathered in the wind,
the easy motion of collected warmth,
cello chords in cacophonous space;

the young come up like thunder
dazzling and harsh as fingernails on slate,
wanting what everyone has always wanted,
mutatis mutandis, how it is:
love and glory, peace, pleasure: power
gaining nothing

but the irrelevancy of their dazed elders
who have only the philosopher's out,
that the greatness of the young will flicker
as it always does among the fickle winds
and most will walk solitary shores, watching
other people's bonfires by the metallic sea.

Bronwen moves through the room
among the elders who have gathered
to celebrate her visit home to this Creek
she's never lived in except as ineluctable
presence in her parents' life, transposed here
as the music segués from Bach's cello

to the whisky-timeless voice of Kevin Quain
and no one is alone on a solitary shore,
elders gathered in a loosely shifting herd
as the bell-mare moves among them like the
shuttle through their loom, like horsehair
giving voice to cello warp and weft,

prodigal of her darkly lambent soul,
cantering rhythms of the Opus 131 implicated
in Bach's graceful courantes, a muscular joy
ringing round in the presence of this room
soundbright when empty and silent, this joy
from the pain of being born that shines

in her mother's eyes. How it is. The clichés
of youth and age unravelled and rewoven
as Joseph's coat in its threads of all colours
and tunings, endlessly. *La fille de mon cœur,*
les fils de mon cœur, the heartstrings
my daughter, while her father shapes verses

in predawn light, perhaps in reconciliation
for a life ill-spent, perhaps in protogeriatric
despair, but finding the first moment of Eden
repeating itself as always to our consternation.
These women. These women, one the lovechild
of myself and the other. These horses in a field.

To find in damp grey morning
the memory of Vimy Ridge blood-orange in Iraq,
this recollection of life given full and warm,
eternally fleeting as love's bright glance.
To find my windswept soul at peace
in my prodigal daughter's casual, heartfelt grace.

9 April 2003

SEEN CLEARLY, THIS WOMAN

for PJ at 56

Seen clearly, this woman
is an epitome in her bones
and silvered hair,
moves like a leopard by Rousseau,
precise, fastidious   languour
implicit in long-muscled elegance
caught stop-frame
as she stoops to conquer
delicacies of her table and guests,
slip seedlings into the earth,
thrash cedar roots from the soil,
scrub catsnot from the oak –
she oils their ears in pragmatic fondness,
collects roadkill for science class
or the anatomical drawing she teaches
the way a conductor leads a choir,
stark gesture of lean beautiful hands
that make carnal music,
flutelike, fierce,
and finger syncopated 64th notes
out of a silver Artley:
flare of hip, poise of ankle,
angle of wrist, cheekbones of the
Lakota Sioux that never got into her genes;
naked in a shallow bath, a nude from
Edward Weston rather than Degas,
practical as peppers, shining as the
sea off Carmel in full lotus as she bends
to cleanse that flexuous silver helmet
she's never coloured back to the raven's wing
still gleaming in her eyes;
warrior soul dark mezzo as her voice
ringing folk canticles through the starry vaults
of her time.

Seen clearly, this woman,
these thirty years since we were young
and without child,
this woman who disdains
arthritis nibbling at those bones,
a decade of brutal menopause.
Seen clearly, this woman
for thirty years the other of my life.
Seen clearly, this woman

End of April

for Peter Trower & the Years

The ghosts of Lillard and Nutter
walked out the bathroom door
at Trower's ancestral pad
where poems yellow the walls like cigarette stains
and Stu Nutter's blood lingers in the carpet
from the last great haemorrhage
when his life finally burst its boozy seams.

Now they haunt my passage home,
echoes of Waylon and John Cash,
Kristofferson and Willie Nelson,
desperados waiting for a train
in this old-gold light sweaty as
October summer in the Roberts Creek bus
past trailer parks to Cemetery Road.

Red, it's been a long time,
rolling south over the ridges from Pendleton
through the heart of Oregon,
Long Creek a highland meadow
we'll never see again.
Hearing for the first time Martina McBride
sing Independence Day through static

all over that radio nowhere
where even the ghost towns have ghost towns
mouldered to archival memory
but you can still find Jim Beam at home,
fiery wet and never lonesome;
McBride declaring freedom as America
never heard it before,

the girl sent to the 4th of July Fair
while her momma blows up the house
the brutal husband and herself –
the biggest fireworks in town
that Independence Day.
The white dove flew up
to the burning blue sky.

Stuart Nutter, tall and lean and outrageous
as Peter O'Toole, drank a bottle of rotgut brandy a day
when he was relatively dry,
reared up from blackout sleep, glass in hand,
to address a gang of desperados in perfect
compound-complex English,
making more sense than most men sober

any time he had the chance. We midnight desperados
knew he'd shot film from airforce planes,
a kid in John Grierson's fledgling NFB
and on through the postwar years,
wrote scripts and newspaper columns,
and probably hadn't drawn a sober breath
in sixty years. Clear-headed as an April dawn.

Stu, you'd charm the legs off an airtight stove,
Pete Trower, and anyone else who came along,
even the wife who threw you out.
Red Lillard sits in ashes in a cedar box
among my books – *Tiger of the Snows,*
The Good Soldier, Descartes. Most of the
desperados gone on the Boot Hill express.

Pretty mom wheels her infant down the forest road
this bus rolls along to End of April Cedar Grove,
sundappled all the day. Ebon-curled sexpot
pulls the bell and swings plush hips
out the doors, strides into the old grave yard
as though she too were going home.

Blue Light for Susan

Susan McCaslin in sapphire light
a visitation
Hildegard of Eibingen might have seen
or been –
madonna pietà
from the collarbones up   sexy as Cher
naked face of the incarnation
come to visit at the hour of the wolf,
speaking silently
the ineffable
the presence,
as though god had said
When the world speaks,
listen.

Al's Shack

for Al MacLachlan

Al's new shack looks out through poplar tops
at Keats and Bowen over the old-coast Eden
of Gibsons Harbour; wind shimmers
the poplar leaves, a flapper's tassels,
Biederbecke blowing scat notes by the bay.
Christy noses double-distilled agave juice
pale peridot green, that elegant schnozz
from a Charlie Rich blues, shares out shots
to toast Al's pad and his own hop to T.O.
on a WestJet bird; slops drops to tequila-finish
the perfume of Al's fir septuagint floors, a
wry Mose Allison grin bending the long notes
of his phyz, improbable bristlecone pine
out of South Philly and a thousand outports since.
The face of a man who knows Parchment Farm.

Lady in red blows through Al's door like sunshine
at midnight in the afternoon blaze: Cher,
who says, "And it's really my name. Maybe
it's really her name too," when I say it takes
quite a woman to carry that name these days,
as she indelibly does, poplar-slim female note
wafting darkly through scarlet drapery, a woman
of fifty who'll never lose seventeen, walnut-sheen
hair, beautiful feet at one end of forever legs,
face brilliant with the patina of the years,
a crying song   I've yet to hear her sing. This place
breeds time into emollients of timeless grace,
men and women like old houses and boats
and the endless benign bewilderment of trees,
supple and tough as yesteryear leather, cedar withes.

Trower sits in the middle of Al's couch, ballasting down
with beer as though he were at home, as he is everywhere.
The peridot tequila takes his head off the way good dope do,
bookended by me and Cher – maybe as good as it gets
when you're down so long with most of the desperados
gone and the nearest in your life pinned by the pincers
of the crab. Pete Trower who came for just one beer
to celebrate Al's new pad and his pal Jim Christy's trip,

the man who never touches hard stuff anymore,
starts seeing poems in the air, ineluctable touch
of the woman   shoulder and ploughshare hip,
me his pal the other side of everything, Charlie Rich
and Kevin Quain singing the blues for Gibsons Harbour
Pete's looked at and lived these sixty years. She takes
him home; I guide him down the stairs; Cher takes

Pete's hand, holds it high to promenade elegance
onto Gibsons Way as though it were Kensington Road
before the Albert Hall. Al's misplaced his camera, stoned
as a coot; Murph's left with Gloria, another crying song
gone girlish; Christy has that look, '40s Screen Gem desperado
waiting for a plane; calm Bradley stops twitching about
the meeting he's schedded for seven; I run for a bus that's late
as the Wonderland rabbit. Waiting around the curve
of Gibsons Way I can hear them hooting like kids on the porch
baptising Al's new shack; then Christy appears, the leading man
bouncing jaunty in hotlicks shirt and slacks, across the road
and through the poplars to fuel up the fridge from Gramma's
Beer & Wine, 'cause the party's gearing up for evening shift
in late May's long lubricious light, and Cher's coming back
to sing the blues, Gibsons seabreeze in Al's new ageless shack.

AMY DUNDAS (1973–2003)

She rode with a gathered abandon
known only to horses;
beat Mario Deslauriers and Box Car Willie
in a double-slalom at Spruce, aboard Fantasia
who flew like an ungulate angel
and would as like have gone over the moon
but for Amy's sprung steel leg and hand
and balance and eye for the next jump and
the next jump and the next jump endlessly
until the last.
Fanny loved to win. Ame Dundas
knew how.

Blonde angel,
killed by the horse she named Menuhin
for the maestro she most admired.
He made the worst mistake a horse can make,
hot for a mare in heat, lashed out an accidental hoof
as his mistress entered the stall, sad Menuhin,
stilled the finest hand that will ever guide him.

She sang Bach on the strings
of the chambered vessel tucked under her chin,
and from her fair throat and blue eyes
brilliant as flax in the sun.
I watched you chewing grass-ends, Ame,
one summer on Milners' farm
as you were just gathering womanhood
like the spirit of Sherry Dawn,

and you asking me to talk sometime
of that life-long event called love –
"How do I find a nice man with a good saddle?"
you smiled and said. Well, that'll be an endless
conversation now, though you did, last summer,
and he stands like a man who caught the wind,
empty handed and touched by a soaring joy
half human half equine in this steel-thewed
second-sighted woman gone forever young.
Bereft,
as am I, left with Casals tuning the spheres
to this unthinkable absence.

FINAL THINGS

Cedar Grove: Mourning Amy

Shadows deepen
in the corner of the room
between two open windows
where climbing roses in middle red
and foxgloves middle fuchsia
sprawl across what I see,
like the opulent epaulettes of god,
to keep the world balanced
and still, as though,
among the complex greens
from lime to dark sequoia,
bourgeois decoration had received
imprimatur from on high
in this time after death
and the gypsy foxglove
been accorded noble station
in the vegetal panoply.

Dawn

Alone with birdsong as the year turns away
toward the long darkness six months on
and we bask in the summer's blaze, knowing
it's a brief whisper to goldengrove unleaving
and knowing too it's ourselves we mourn for,
these margarets we are; and the gone remembered
– that blonde hair flying one last time forever.

ICONIC

among cedars, a globe of light spins golden
in summer sun, anachronistic
as an astrolabe or Harrison's nautical clock –
oblivious to all,
a life neither mine nor yours nor ours
but a will-o'-the-wisp, a ball
of St Elmo's fire. We can hear it singing,
without human meaning, without
human feeling – a foreign song:
what Wallace Stevens knew
by the end of his years at least.
And so we ask, Where does it turn?
as the year turns away from high solstice
and we turn away from the latest
golden friend gone under,
and we recall her making squirrel noises
like a five-year-old, never giving her
name when she called on the phone,
annoyed if we didn't
                                        instantly
know who *Hello* was.
And we wonder.   And we mourn
for joy endless as death
in the globe's turning
under the sun among cedars.

Εσχατος

It explodes
like a jump horse going over an eight-foot wall
and it's only a day.
The horse hangs in the sky, eternal
instant of the godforce stamped into eyeblue sky
and into the brain –
four-hooved flight beyond the impossible,
phar lap, which means lightning
and was the name of a horse
murdered for beating the best
America had to offer.
And it's only a day. By midafternoon,
so still at 30° in the shade nothing seems to move,
not even the strip-loin bands of cirrus in the sky,
not even the children running beneath the trees.
And not the jump horse
that will never come down.

ENDNOTES

EPIGRAPH

The epigraph is excerpted from "Kensington Pub Thursday" in *The Last Trip to Oregon* (Ronsdale Press: Vancouver, 2002).

MUSTAGH TOWER

The "last blue mountain barred with snow" occurs in James Elroy Flecker's "The Golden Journey to Samarkand" (*Collected Poems,* Martin Secker: London, 1916), as an image for the obstacles to be surmounted by the pilgrims on their journey. Ralph Barker used *The Last Blue Mountain* as the title for his 1959 account of a tragic assault on Mt. Haramosh in the Karakoram (Chatto & Windus: London).

The Hindi/Nepalese word *namaste,* accompanied by eye contact with hands pressed together at the heart and a brief bow, is a traditional greeting which can be interpreted as "I honour that place in you where the whole universe resides. And when I am in that place in me and you are in that place in you, there is only one of us."

10 SEPTEMBER

Harbertonford is a village in South Devon.

SUMMER RAIN

Gottfried Benn (1886–1956) was a German Expressionist poet who served in both world wars as an army pathologist. The italicized lines are from "What's Bad," Christopher Middleton's translation of Benn's "Was schlimm ist?" in *Primal Vision: Selected Writings* (New Directions: New York, [1960]).

FROM GOWER POINT TO IRVINES LANDING

Maudzi is a phonetic spelling of the Joual pronunciation of *maudit.*

BEACH AVENUE

The Stevens is from his "Connoisseur of Chaos" in *Collected Poems* (Alfred A. Knopf: New York, 1954).

PREECE

"Babylon by the Bay" is a pejorative term for the city of Vancouver – coined, I believe, by Allan Fotheringham. Allister MacGillivray's "Song for the Mira" immortalizes that estuarial Cape Breton river and the town of Marion Bridge.

CHRISTMAS 2002

The the. These are the final two words of Stevens's "The Man on the Dump" in *Collected Poems.*

Dogs Euthanized after Savaging Shenica

Shenica is the name of a fourteen-year-old girl attacked by two Mastiff-Rottweilers which had wandered out an unlatched gate.

Gumboot Nation

The independent Nation of Roberts Creek, known as The Gumboot Nation, was declared by Creekers during hard times in the 1980s. They later crowned Doug and Helen Roy King and Queen to honour them for their contribution to the community. Hence, the Quingdom of Roberts Creek.

Hubert Evans (1892–1986), an early settler at Roberts Creek, was one of British Columbia's first significant fiction writers. His best-known novel is *Mist on the River.*

The News

This poem was written at the turning of the year 2002–2003, a month before *Columbia* burned up in the sky.

The Axle of History

The Stevens is from his "Continual Conversation with a Silent Man" in *Collected Poems.*

Ronald Blythe's *Akenfield: Portrait of an English Village* (Penguin Press: Middlesex, 1969) is a landmark of social history. It consists of interviews with residents of this Suffolk village, such as the wheelwright Jubal Merton, and commentary by the author.

Now and Then

Jon Furberg was an influential thinker, writer and teacher in the Vancouver countercultural literature of the 1970s exemplified by Pulp Press, of which he was a seminal *geist.* Although he published little, he touched many. Furberg's *Prepositions for Remembrance Day* (Pulp: Vancouver, 1981) and *Anhaga* (Arsenal Pulp: Vancouver, 1983), an "interpretation" from the Anglo-Saxon of *The Wanderer,* remain with me always – the bevelled edges of insight and language. Jon died of cancer, with elegant compassion for those preparing to mourn him.

Paxil and I

The American poet Theodore Roethke committed suicide in 1963. His *Collected Poems* was published by Doubleday in 1966. The lines quoted here, in the early part of the poem, are from "Meditation in Hydrotherapy"; "the pure serene of memory in one man" is from "The Far Field", title poem of Roethke's last book. The geese "who cried, in goose, Alas?" are from John Crowe Ransom's poem "Bells for John Whiteside's Daughter". The first comma and the question mark are not.

THE C-WORD AS REDEMPTION

The William Butler Yeats lines are from "Crazy Jane Talks with the Bishop" in *The Winding Stair and Other Poems* (Macmillan: London, 1933).

FOREST GUBBINAL

"Gubbinal" is the title of a Wallace Stevens poem with the refrain "The world is ugly, / And the people are sad." The Eumenides, "the Kindly Ones," is a propitiatory name for the Erinyes, avenging figures in Greek Mythology often called the Furies in English.

LOONS CALLING IN GEORGIA STRAIT

Montana Lake is in the middle of nowhere in central British Columbia. Mt. Arrowsmith is a dominant, rampart-like peak of the Vancouver Island Ranges.

THE GHOST OF ALAN MOOREHEAD

Alan Moorehead's three-volume account of the North African campaign of World War II was republished in 2001 by Penguin as one volume under the title *Desert War. A Year of Battle* is volume two of the trilogy. The British 7th Armoured Division earned the sobriquet "Desert Rats" for its heroic exploits against Erwin Rommel's Afrika Korps on the sands and stony plains of the Western Desert. Like a battle flag, the nickname is permanent.

PRODIGAL DAUGHTER

9 April is the anniversary of the Canadian assault on Vimy Ridge in 1917, an event which changed the nation's relationship to the world. In 2003, it is the day of the "fall" of Baghdad, which is likely to change the relationship of the world to itself.

SEEN CLEARLY, THIS WOMAN

Artley is a maker of flutes, piccolos, clarinets and other wind instruments.

BLUE LIGHT FOR SUSAN

St. Hildegard was a twelfth-century German visionary and prophet. As part of a correspondence on mysticism, Susan McCaslin sent me a copy of Hildegard's "True Trinity in True Unity," an iconographic image showing "a sapphire-blue prophetic figure surrounded by a brilliant light ... suspended before a fiery golden disk." The background is midnight blue. The italicized lines closing this poem are a variation on the end of Susan's "White Meditation" (*At the Mercy Seat,* Ronsdale Press: Vancouver, 2003).

AL'S SHACK

Keats and Bowen are islands at the mouth of Howe Sound. "Parchment Farm" is the title of a Mose Allison song describing life on the infamous prison farm in the American South.

AMY DUNDAS

In the early 1990s, Mario Deslauriers and Box Car Willie were an elite equestrian jumping pair in Canada, next to Ian Miller and Big Ben. Amy (although considered a promising young rider) and her reclaimed thoroughbred Fantasia were given no chance even to reach the final of this long, single-knockout competition at Spruce Meadows.

Amy's nickname was "Ame." Sherry Dawn was a chestnut-and-white pinto pony mare, dam of several good-quality jumpers, ridden by Amy and subsequently my daughter Bronwen to win many competitions.

ICONIC

John Harrison was the inventor of the first reliable marine chronometer. The italicized lines are from Stevens's "Of Mere Being," in *Opus Posthumous* (Alfred A. Knopf: New York, 1957).

Εσχατος

The title is a Greek word meaning "the uttermost" or "the last," root of the English word *eschatology,* the study of final things.

About the Author

Vancouver-born **George Payerle** is a poet, novelist, translator and editor whose parents immigrated from Hungary after WW I. His first novel, *the afterpeople* (Anansi, 1970), formed part of his master's thesis at the University of British Columbia. *Unknown Soldier* was published by Macmillan in 1987 and remains a definitive expression of a combat veteran's experience in civilian life. Payerle's fiction, poems and translations have found periodical and anthology publication over the past three decades in North America, Europe and Australia. His first full-length book of poems, *The Last Trip to Oregon* (Ronsdale, 2002), memorialized the death of his friend, the poet Charles "Red" Lillard. George and his wife, Phyllis, now live in Roberts Creek on the Sunshine Coast. They have one daughter, Bronwen. *Alterations* constitutes a celebration of Payerle's new life as an urban refugee among cedar trees.

About the Artist

Deborah DeWit Marchant is an Oregon painter, pastellist and photographer whose work has been shown throughout the United States as well as in Canada and Europe. DeWit's book *Traveling Light* (Impassio Press: Seattle, 2003), a photgrapher's memoir, presents a remarkable visual/philosophical insight into the mind of a woman whose camera is an extension of her eye and fey spirit.